HUMAN RESOURCES

ADULT
COLORING BOOK

Enjoying this book?

Please leave a review because we would love to know your thoughts, feedback, and opinions to create better paper products for you!

Thank you so much for your support.

KEEP
CALM
AND
CALL
HR

YOU'RE AN AWESOME HR SPECIALIST KEEP THAT SHIT UP.

It would be a great career
if you didn't have to deal
with people.

I DO PAYROLL YOU SHOULD BE NICE TO ME

NOTHING SURPRISES ME ANYMORE I WORK IN HR

I'M IN HR
I CAN'T FIX CRAZY
BUT I CAN
DOCUMENT IT

I work in HR for the gossip

49% HR SPECIALIST
51% BADASS

I'M AN
HR SPECIALIST
...AND I'M IN IT
FOR THE MONEY

WILL GIVE
HR ADVICE
FOR
coffee

WORLD'S BEST HR SPECIALIST

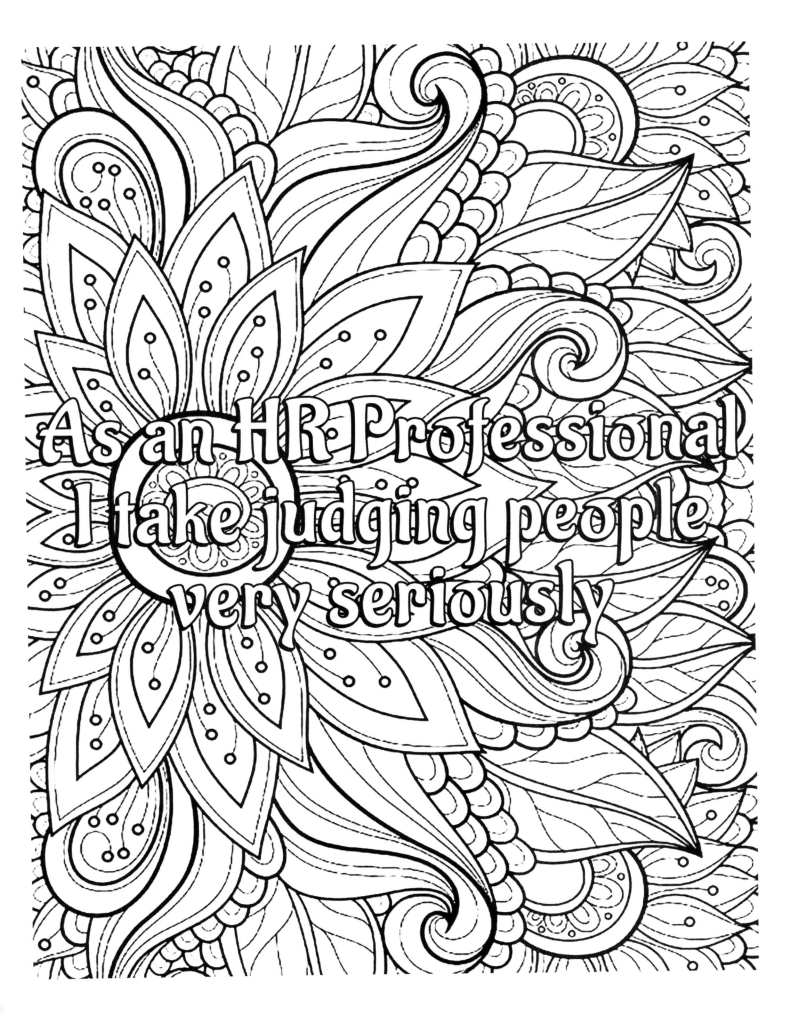